# Decorate Rich

*Creating a Fabulous Look for Less*

# Decorate Rich

## Creating a Fabulous Look for Less

### Jo Packham

Sterling Publishing Co., Inc. New York
A Sterling/Chapelle Book

# Chapelle Ltd.

Owner: Jo Packham

Editor: Linda Orton

Staff: Areta Bingham, Kass Burchett, Marilyn Goff,
Holly Hollingsworth, Susan Jorgensen, Barbara Milburn,
Karmen Quinney, Leslie Ridenour, Cindy Stoeckl,
Gina Swapp, Sara Toliver

Photography: Kevin Dilley, for Hazen Imaging, Inc.
Phil Cordova, Cordova Photography
Luciana Pampalone, Luciana Pampalone Studio
Scot Zimmerman for Scott Zimmerman Photography
Robert Perron
Sue Henshaw, title page
Joe Coca, Joe Coca Photography

Library of Congress Cataloging-in-Publication

Packham, Jo
    Decorate rich : creating a fabulous look for less / Jo Packham
        p. cm.
    "A Sterling/Chapelle book."
    Includes index.
  ISBN 0-8069-6267-4
    1. Interior decoration. I. Title.

NK1980 .P25 2001
747--dc21                                                00-053790

10 9 8 7 6 5 4 3 2

A Sterling/Chapelle Book

First paperback edition published in 2002 by
Sterling Publishing Company, Inc.
387 Park Avenue South, New York, N.Y. 10016
© 2001 by Chapelle Ltd.
Distributed in Canada by Sterling Publishing
C/o Canadian Manda Group, One Atlantic Avenue, Suite 105
Toronto, Ontario, Canada M6K 3E7
Distributed in Great Britain and Europe by Chrysalis Books
64 Brewery Road, London N7 9NT, England
Distributed in Australia by Capricorn Link (Australia) Pty. Ltd.
P.O. Box 704, Windsor, NSW 2756 Australia

Printed in China
All Rights Reserved

Sterling ISBN 0-8069-6267-4  Hardcover
            0-8069-7549-0  Paperback

Every effort has been made to ensure that all of the information in this book is accurate.

If you have any questions or comments, please contact:

Chapelle Ltd., Inc.
P.O. Box 9252
Ogden, UT 84409

Phone: (801) 621-2777
FAX: (801) 621-2788
e-mail: chapelle@chapelleltd.com
website: www.chapelleltd.com

I was born in Ogden, Utah, to the parents to whom I owe my dreams. All of their, and my life, they have been honest, good people who worked hard and taught their two daughters to be and do the same. My mother, who is wiser than her educated years, made me believe that there wasn't anything I couldn't accomplish—I simply needed to learn how. And not only could I accomplish it, but I could do it with a champagne appetite (which I inherited from my father) on a beer budget. This, I believe, is when I first began to learn to *Decorate Rich.* I am certain it all started when my mother made her prom dress from the living room curtains—and all of my school years, she created the same magic for me.

I graduated with honors in Art from the University of California at Sacramento. Upon graduation, I returned home and opened Apple Arts, a retail store that sold art supplies. I decided the retail industry wasn't for me and started The Vanessa-Ann Collection with very little money, a good idea, and an uncontrollable passion.

That was twenty-one years ago, in which time I have been blessed with a son, a daughter, and a son-in-law, whom I adore more than words can describe. I have been honored with YWCA's first "Business of the Year" Award, have received numerous awards within my industry for prize-winning photography, and I have traveled around the country teaching and consulting. I have authored thirteen of my own publications and have been responsible for the publication of approximately 200 titles, which have been designed and written by over 100 individual authors.

I still live in Ogden in a home that was built in 1929, which I am renovating with my husband. We live there with his garden and his aquarium, my daughter's five cats, and my son's dog.

I have been blessed with both the "best of times and the worst of times," which I believe is needed to make us all understand and appreciate all that life has to offer.

# Table of Contents

# On the Wall

**Decorating rich** on the wall is a perfect place to begin. It is the foundation for decorating. Everything is placed on the wall or in front of it. It can be the center of attention and focus or a subtle backdrop. It can be all of the decoration that is needed in a room or it can be the perfect accessory. Whichever you choose—it can be where you begin when you start *decorating rich!*

The finish on the walls in your home can be that which is the art that you hang upon them. Each finish can be so unique, so one-of-a-kind that those who see it will think each wall could—and probably should—be a signed original.

This book is not here to teach the techniques for painting on walls but rather to give the inspiration. There are countless wonderful technique books on faux finishes if you wish to be the "artist in residence," or professionals you can hire who can create the look you want—just show them a picture.

By turning your walls into art, it creates a focal point that requires no additions. It can, therefore, be a very inexpensive way to make an entire room a masterpiece.

Unusual faux finishes do not necessarily have to be on an entire wall, they can be perfectly placed in areas that are smaller and sometimes partially hidden. As an unanticipated detail they take decorating from the ordinary to the unexpected extraordinary.

*Lower left:* Bring the beauty of autumn into your room in places that are small, yet as important as the leaves that change colors on the trees.

Do not feel bound by traditional faux finishes, those that you see in every magazine article on new and innovative decorating styles or in every book on the newest painting techniques. Create something that is truly new—that is distinctively you. Everything you see can be re-created on your walls. It will probably use the same techniques as those used in established faux finishes, but may be a new combination of two or three techniques, or an unusual use of colors or supplies.

The most unusual finishes on these pages were created with large individual stencils which were made and then used by overlapping each other. The paints were diluted to differing degrees of opaqueness with glazing solutions. It is dramatic—time consuming, but easy and inexpensive.

11

Fill your home with light and color, and shades of blue. You need not live by the deep blue sea or always have a clear blue sky to enjoy part of that which they offer.

The color blue is heavenly, royal, pristine, dignified, and deeply prized. It is calming, sensitive, orderly, and quiet. It represents faith, trust, and integrity. It is a favorite for almost everyone.

When you decide to add shades of blue to your decorating, you can do so on entire walls or in small sections. You can combine it with shades of yellow or grey, or you can add swirls of white and black.

Whatever you do, wherever you put it, whatever colors you add to it, blue is a color of which you will rarely grow tired. It is the color of that which we wish for most in our lives.

13

Orange may be a secondary color on a wheel-of-color, but for some it is definitely their primary color of choice.

Yellow and red are mixed to create orange, so naturally it is a color that is warm, rich, strong, vital, intense, and so dramatic. Orange is also extroverted, expansive, cheerful, contemporary, and young.

Orange brings the sun from the outside in. It is the warmth of the evening fire on the walls that surround you, it is the promise of a beautiful day no matter the season or the temperature outside, it is that which fills your home with the light and color and beauty that inspires you. It is a color that alone can warm your body, as well as your mind and your soul.

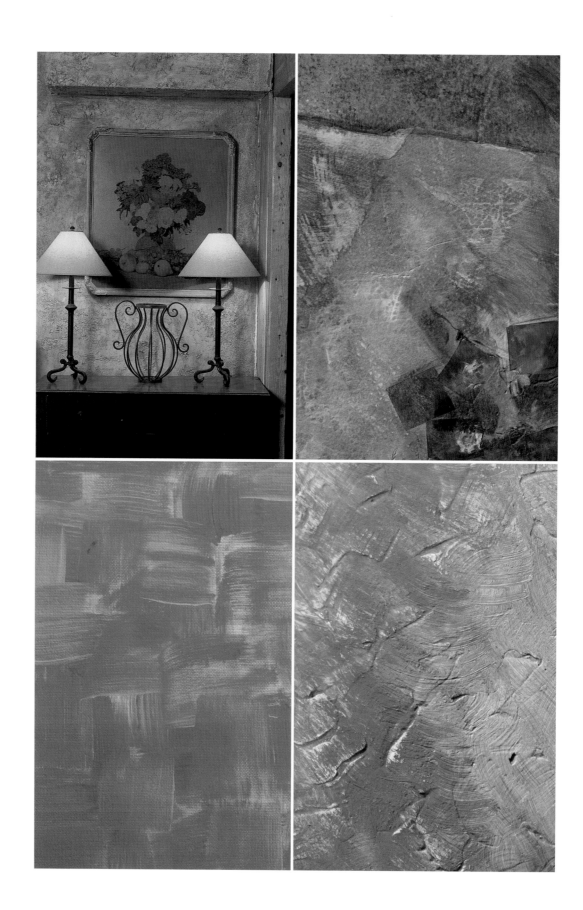

Orange in all of its varia-tions is one of the colors of nature. Its vibrant shades can be those that make up the color of the sunset. When it is combined with brown, it changes to rust—the color of the earth that has been warmed by the sun, or metal that has been gently aged by rainy days followed by the rays of the sun.

Cover your walls with rust-ed pieces of tin—it will add a touch of nature.

Those ordinary everyday "things" can be used to create almost anything on your walls. Here is an example *(upper right)* of how brown paper bags were used to create illusions of stone like those in European country homes. Bags were used *(upper left)* to re-create aged cement walls like those in a Tuscany villa. The example of the leaves *(below)*, done with silk ivy leaves, masking tape, and antique medium, adds a new measure to an old finish.

To cover your wall with brown postal paper or paper bags, simply tear the paper into desired sized pieces. Decoupage paper onto the wall, and sponge light brown paint over the bags in a circular motion. You can add motifs cut from fabric or paper onto the paper before painting. To make it look like stone, fill areas between faux stones with grout.

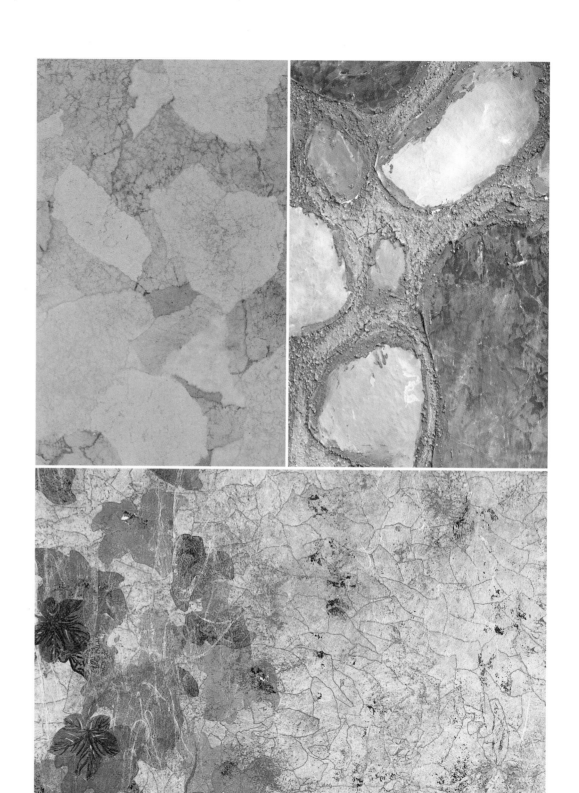

Stenciling or painting on walls and doors is another traditional technique that can add anything from sophisticated ease to simple homespun luxury to your home. Such designs will enhance your decorating style in unexpected subtle, yet profound ways. If you like that which is orderly and precise, use a stencil; if light and airy is more your palate, use a paintbrush and eliminate all patterns.

These are works of art that you will grow more fond of with each passing day—and they will make any room complete. No need for additional expensive paintings or tapestries—the painted walls are simply enough.

18

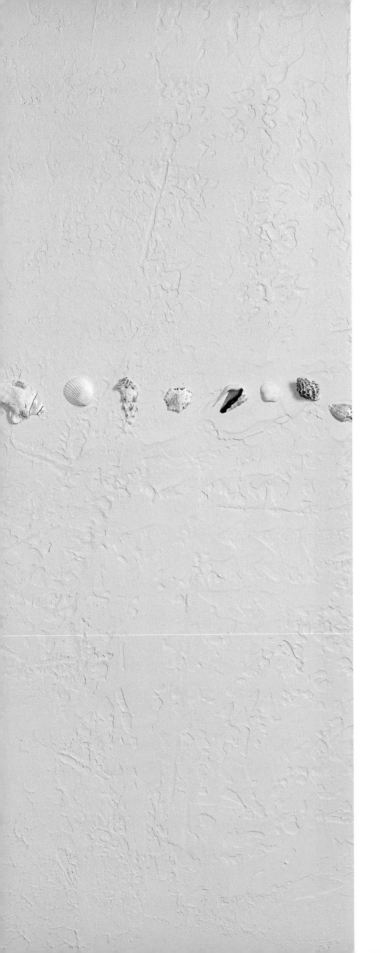

Elements of style can range from the most simplistic to the overly ornate. In our homes, some of us like that which is overdone, that which represents maybe not all but most of that which we love. While others of us—or maybe all of us in just different parts of our home—like something simple, yet memorable. Whichever style you choose and use, it can look like you *decorate rich.*

Here are three examples of walls that are easy and inexpensive to create, yet add elements of style.

*Facing page, upper left:* Walls such as these that were carved by artisans in the palaces and country homes of the wealthy in Europe can easily be re-created by simply gluing plastic or plaster forms and borders to your walls. The seams are then covered with caulking or drywall compound, and the wall is painted. Use your imagination—anything from outdoor plaster busts to plastic angel wall plaques can be used.

*This page and facing page, lower left:* These simple wall treatments were created by texturing the wall with drywall compound and then, while still wet, small pieces of collected beach glass or seashells were added. (If the compound will not hold the collected pieces, they may have to be glued in place with a strong adhesive.)

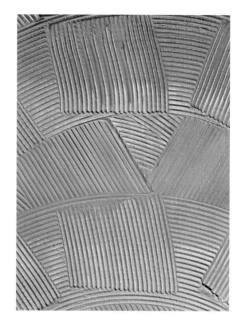

Concrete walls in a garden can be a backdrop that is as much a piece of art for your flowers as those in the theater are for the actors.

Paint them with drips or combs or crayons, then partially cover them with vines or roses or collected treasures.

It matters not that such pieces will weather—it makes them as natural as they are beautiful.

Not only do we have walls that surround us, support us, and protect us on the inside of our homes, but we have them on the outside as well. These walls, that are the first to tell visitors who we are, need not be standard brick or concrete; they too can be works of art.

If you live in an older ordinary brick home, why not make the brick look weathered and aged—like those homes in Europe that have stood for hundreds of years. Or, if your home has cement walls that surround the driveway, splashes of paint can color them in warm natural hues.

Such finishes are not right for everyone, but they are ones that can dramatically enhance something otherwise old and unwanted.

## On the Wall with Dimension

On the wall also means that which you hang on the wall. But, if you are intent on *decorating rich,* that means hanging something in a manner that is unexpected. If you decorate with the traditional, it is much more difficult to look unusual.

*Facing page, upper left:* Here a ribbon wreath was hung on a plant stand rather than directly on the wall. It adds an element that is lightweight, refined, and silky soft.

*Facing page, lower left:* In this instance, the wreath was hung directly from the coatrack and not to the side of it. There is still room for other ornamental items to hang from the rack, which creates a work of art from something that is thought of mostly as utilitarian and functional.

*Facing page, right:* Use candle wall sconces to hold flower arrangements in place of candles. It is an elegant contradiction full of detail and design.

This looks like a wall vase, but is actually half of a decoupaged wastebasket that has been attached to the wall. Inside, a small vase was placed so that the leaves could be kept as fresh as possible. To make it reflect your decorating tastes even more, attach tassels, beads, or ribbons to hang down from each side. These are hung from a small hook placed in the wall next to the "vase." This is an idea that can be duplicated regardless of your decorating style. Country is as easy to achieve as Victorian or Asian.

One easy way to *decorate rich* is to use groups of things—all of one or combinations. Use your coatrack to hang scarves and hats—so you don't need a picture. Create a "box" in your workroom and hang your ribbons. They are not only beautiful, colorful, and inspirational, but now, easier to use.

Hang your favorite hats with your treasured photographs and prints. Hang mirrors in a grouping—we usually only think to group pictures—or hang scarves over a mirror. This will be the perfect reflection of your new *decorating rich* style. Do not be afraid to group things, different or alike.

## From Functional to Decorative

*Decorating rich* can mean taking something utilitarian, something that every home has that is used every single day, and presenting it in a way that makes it important. Such a display need not be expensive—it simply needs to be unexpected. A little extra attention needs to be paid to the details. It should create a moment when a common sight becomes as romantic as a sonnet, as artistic as a Van Gogh, as nontraditional as a study in contrasts.

You need not use ordinary towel racks from which to hang your towels. Use whatever you like—simply add a hook or two. And add items you love, whatever they may be.

*Facing page and left:* Here are examples of taking something that we all live with day in and day out, and turning it into a simple luxury that will enhance your everyday life-style.

27

If you are hesitant to hang your towels from anything but traditional towel racks, add something else that is sophisticated. Overlap towels and tie them together with beaded tassels, or put a basket filled with towels on the floor directly underneath your hanging towels. Even add bottles to your arrangement on the floor—bottles empty or filled. Use bath oils and salts and then drape tiny beaded bags filled with magic potions around the bottle's neck. With such attention to detail, you will be taking care of the spirit as well as the body.

*Below:* These four towels are hung from curtain tieback hardware. They were purchased at a drapery store on a closeout, so one was the same price as four. To build on this creative thought, one towel of a contrasting color was used and a favorite tassel from MacKenzie-Childs Ltd. was added for sheer effect.

## On the Window

What is so wonderful about decorating on the wall is that there are so many surfaces and so many options. Here "on the wall" is in reference to window coverings. In the *upper left,* a metal filagree was found in a garden shop and used to hang drapery panels. They were hung by an inside door in a hallway—an unexpected surprise. In the *lower left,* cabinet doors with copper-lined tree cutouts were used similar to shutters. And *above,* tin ceiling panels were trimmed with fringe and nailed to the molding. In each instance, something practical was simply made clever, stylish, and unique— which is the definition of *decorating rich!*

When a discussion of decorating styles is entered into, there will be as many "popular" styles as there are people involved in the discussion. For some, the only acceptable style is that of the Terrance Conran style—sleek, minimalist, and sophisticated. For others, the belief that "too much is never enough" is that by which they both decorate and live. Here is a collector of vintage pieces who is compelled to display all of which she owns. What is the fun of having something, if it is tucked away in a drawer? She hangs towels, teapots, and aprons from her windows—the more she has, the better it is and the more she loves it. She says, "It is easy to change on a whim and makes me smile!"

31

## On the Ceiling

A small "reach" for decorating on the wall is to use the ceiling as an extension of the wall. And on the ceiling is the lighting.

In the days before us, the candle's flame not only gave the only available light, but also set the mood. Everything was softened and surrounded by the warm glow of the candlelight. Today, we often forget to be creative with our lighting. We feel compelled to purchase expensive fixtures to create any kind of a mood; but to *decorate rich* one need not buy expensive lights—you just need to start seeing all that is around you as a light fixture.

*Facing page, left:* Metal garden gates were "framed" into the ceiling and small lights were hung.

*Facing page, right:* A discarded metal chandelier was strung with glass beads and the ceiling was painted to draw attention upward.

Just because designers and manufacturers say that certain lights are for out-of-doors, dining rooms, entry ways, etc., does not mean that is what they should always be used for. Here inexpensive outdoor lights were grouped together and hung in the bathroom. They were a more creative touch than traditional bathroom lights.

A stained-glass window purchased from an "antique" store was hung on the ceiling to add rich patterns to the light falling onto the bed. The window you purchase may be one that is old, valuable, intricate in design, and abundant with color; or it may be a new window with simply beveled clear glass pieces that act as prisms casting rainbows on the walls of your bedroom. The options and the results are as varied as there are windows available.

## Cupboards on the Wall

Also included in decorating on the wall are the cupboards that often cover most of the walls in our homes. They are necessary, but often unimaginative. Why not cut out designs in the cupboard doors to continue your decorating theme? Here aspen leaves were cut into each door to add a little touch of something special.

Cupboard doors need not always be made of wood. Cover your cupboards with your favorite pieces of fabric or lace. In this way, they can be easily changed for the season, the holiday, or just for the mood you are in. This is simply another example of how *decorating rich* becomes easy, affordable, and creative.

## Fireplace on the Wall

It seems that almost everyone would like to have a fireplace in their home; not only for the holidays and cold winter nights, but for all of the chilly mornings that come with days that are as crisp as a granny smith apple. And what about simply wanting a fireplace, so that the mantle can be used to display family heirlooms, or to be the center of the room where family and friends are gathered?

If you do not have a fireplace and your physical structure cannot support a "real one", create the illusion of one. Purchase the mantle and outer trimmings you have always wanted, and decorate it as you will. You may find that these fireplaces will be used more and admired more than one that is actually functional.

A fireplace that is used as a piece of art can be an area where you do that which you wouldn't dare do anywhere else is your home. You can decorate around a theme, you can use both the mantle and the fireplace opening as a display case for your collections, or you can overdo it and design that which most of your friends simply will not understand. The dog pedestal with the porcelain purebred lying on top is definitely not something I would create in my home, but I do understand why the artist loves it as much as she does.

## Art on the Wall

The most traditional of decorating on a wall is that of hanging pictures; however, when *decorating rich,* even those become unpredictable. The sunflower picture on the *left* is one of my favorite. It hangs in the dining room of a friend and is her least expensive, yet most valuable possession. When she and her husband completed their garden, they had a large garden party, inviting friends and family. On one of the picnic tables outside, she spread a piece of painter's canvas and placed a variety of brushes and paints. During the evening, each guest painted one sunflower on the canvas— the result is extraordinary.

To the *upper right,* a second friend hung two large pictures on either side of the doorway that leads from her kitchen/dining area down her hallway. The pictures were painted to go together by a young art student who didn't charge much, but could just as easily have been two halves of one large poster.

To the *lower right,* a hand-painted scarf was hung in a door that, because it is left uncovered, becomes part of the wall. The scarf is a beautiful piece that is usually taken down and worn on special evenings out but, upon returning home, finds a place to be shown off—not hidden in a drawer.

41

Oftentimes there are large wall areas in our homes that we want to be richly covered in layers of romantic embroidery and fine venetian lace, but we simply cannot afford such an extravagance. Here, a friend framed the months of her favorite calender. This particular calender was purchased from an artist in a little shop in Soho. It was very much a bargain because it was not acquired until August of the year for which it was made. Such a calender can be handmade—a project every January for the members of your family. Each person can create the month of their birth and the other months can be divided by important occasions that are yet to be celebrated. A second option is to use the pages of a book or calender painted by your favorite artist or illustrator. I created just such a piece with the pages of a children's book whose illustrations I love.

*Right:* An old door was framed with mirrors and hung on an inside wall with a favorite garden plaque. Surrounded by fresh plants, it is perfect for a kitchen or a garden room.

*Below:* This window faced onto a neighbor's fence, so the window was replaced with french doors paneled with mirror in place of glass. The wall was faux-finished and two identical sconces were hung on either side. What was once unwanted is now "essential."

# On the Table

**Decorating rich** on the table is so very important because tables are the stages which we set. They are miniature theaters of social behavior where a substantial percentage of everyday life is played out.

It is here that stories are told, that problems are solved, that love blossoms or withers, that careers are made or undone, that fortunes are founded or squandered. The table is a place for sharing, for enjoyment, for celebration, for wit, for discovery, for art, or intrigue. It is here that we set the props that forecast the order of events, and imply that which we want stated.

Anyone can set a table. The success of a table setting depends not on financial considerations, but on having a personal style. A style that is exhibited in an idea that needs to be developed, a story that needs to be told, or an occasion that needs to be celebrated.

Each table setting is, in a way, a self-portrait of the painter that creates it, an autobiography of the writer who sets the stage and tells the stories.

What makes a great table setting? The best table settings, it could be said, are those that reflect the meal, the season, and the occasion. A mixture of old and new, contemporary and traditional, formal and informal, cluttered or sparse—it matters not. What is important is that no detail escapes your attention. On the table especially, where there is so little room, it is the attention to details that matters most.

Tables are set for many reasons. Some for the mundane routines of every day, some for the family meal, some for a special occasion, some for a party of twenty, and some for just the two of you.

It seems to me that everything significant in our lives has always been announced, celebrated, discussed, and analyzed around the dinner table—which is why my table is always decorated or set in some way.

We bring family and friends together around the table, we give thanks for our blessings around the table, and we share the most memorable days of our lives around the table.

Tables should be set for family and guests to enjoy good food, good conversation, and great settings with just the right mixture of abandonment and restraint.

Having a party to celebrate back-to-school or a favorite teacher's birthday? Use chalkboards! What fun the students and adults alike will have before, during, and after the meal . . . and when the meal is cleared away, take the blackboards and hang them where they will be used again and again. And don't forget to take them down for the next lunch-time snack with friends.

48

The accessories that are used on the table need not be as expensive as the designer plates that they adorn. These pieces, created by MacKenzie-Childs Ltd., are perfect, indeed, when vegetables from the garden or fresh flowers are added. Such decorating will not stay fresh for hours, but it will last through one meal if it is set on the table immediately before dinner is to be served.

The serving of dessert requires only the most subtle of decoration. With the scent of freshly brewed coffee, rich gourmet chocolate and almond, or fresh fruit pie, a visual accent of flowers, lace, fresh fruit, cinnamon sticks, or nuts is all that is needed—but it is needed. Imagine if you will, how very ordinary the chocolate pudding to the *right* becomes without the lace and flowers and a dollop of whipping cream with fresh berries.

It is the little things which mean so much to so many.

Ideas for centerpieces abound. They reflect the best of the season, the theme of party, and the guests who will be partaking. Why not "paint" a picture of the meal for the table's centerpiece? Take a large frame, place it in the center of the table and arrange inside those items that highlight the meal to be served. If the meal is a seated occasion for four, frames can even be used for placemats. Place fabric or prints behind the glass, cover the back with felt, and set the dishes, silverware, and napkins inside the frame.

*Decorating rich* means using the same table, the same occasion, the same essentials in many different ways. Change it just a little and it will always look new.

When serving a buffet, have the buffet table become the "piéce de résistance." Create a way of serving food that is an event—they do it in expensive restaurants and so can you. It is easy to place the clams on a cake plate rather than in a bowl, or surround the wine glasses with grapes and candles rather than merely lining them up at the end of the table.

Each time you go to a lovely restaurant and the food is displayed in a memorable way, take notes. Or take serving ideas from magazines and duplicate them during your own parties. You need not create all of the ideas yourself; and you do not need fancy serving pieces—use what you have for something that you might not have used it before. A scarf becomes a tablecloth, an ice scoop serves cherries, a fancy bottle is filled with oil and vinegar—you are now worthy of much praise and adoration.

Set your table like a stage. Serve your food as if those who partake are a part of the play. How much better, for not only very special guests, but just for the family to cut their cheese from a mini still life. When food is offered in such a manner, it becomes a delight to all of the senses. Each experience is one that will leave tiny pleasant memories whenever you are thought of. It becomes the catalyst for moments that are ordinary, yet worth celebrating.

## Just the Touch

A small table beside a couch or a favorite chair is made practical when that which it holds are items that are often used. In addition to its practicality, it can be clever, stylish, or worldly simply by adding different items. Whatever you choose, do not be afraid to change them often. I move my pieces from shelf to shelf and table to table every time I dust. By doing so, my household chores become an afternoon in an art gallery, rearranging the pieces that are so loved and admired by so many.

# On the Mantle

Any room with a fireplace is the ultimate retreat. It is a haven for private reflection, a place to create secret dreams, an enclave where evenings can be spent with family and friends. It is here that you can wrap yourself in the quiet of the moment or the laughter that fills the room.

It is here that you are surrounded by those you love, the treasures you have collected, and the warmth of the fire. It is here in an unusually small area that you can create a style that is truly your own. It can be a fireplace mantle that is the essence of simple homespun luxury, a work of art that is the epitome of sophisticated ease, or one which walks the line between sporty and chic. Whatever your style, the mantle above your fireplace is that essential part of your home which welcomes the family back, the child in, and the neighbors over.

The beauty of decorating on the mantle is that it can be so many things to so many people, and it can be so easily and inexpensively changed. In one home, a mantle can be a piece of wood attached to the wall above the fireplace with nothing to adorn it but a few simple treasures. In another home, it can be an elegant piece of decorative woodwork that is full of detail and design, and covered with that which is highly collectible and fragile.

A mantle can set the style of the home in one simple statement. Those who enter will know immediately if you have surrounded yourself with details from the arts-and-crafts era, if you like the outdoors and the feel of a hunting lodge, or if you simply like that which is undefinable, clean, simple, and uncluttered.

*Above:* I like to "tuck" little flowers into small hiding places on top of my mantle. It can be done in such a way that the flowers will stay fresh for days and days. Simply go to your florist, purchase the small water vials that fit neatly on the end of each stem, then trim each flower stem and slip it into the water-filled vial. Tuck the vials towards the back of the mantle and hide them with treasures that you have retrieved from drawers and shelves in back bedrooms.

*Right:* The mantle is one of the best places to display those items that are of higher value. These items can be secured by a wax compound, available at museum stores, and are usually out of reach of little hands. They are oftentimes noticed here more than anywhere else in the house.

*Facing page, lower left:* Beautiful bouquets can be made to last "forever" and always look fresh. Make the main part of the bouquet from silk flowers, then insert a few of your favorite fresh flowers, placed in individual water-filled vials, into the front of the bouquet. All you need do is change the few fresh flowers as necessary.

Do not be afraid to change your mantle with the season, with the holiday, with the celebration of a special occasion, or with a change of mood.

This is the mantle in my home and for me it is the center of all that we love and do. In the spring I decorate my mantle with all of my treasures that I have collected the year before; in the summer on my mantle you will find my vases filled with flowers from the garden, or fruit from the trees, bringing the outside in. During the months of fall, I have candles and baskets and all things that capture the season; and Christmas, of course, has the treasures of the holidays and the stockings for Santa to fill.

My mantle is never the same twice because it is the one area that everyone notices first and remembers last. With its constant changing, my family and friends think I have decorating skills unlimited and a budget that is endless. The truth is that by using that which nature gives freely, arranging the same items in different ways with different accents, and combining my junk-store finds with my collectible pieces, the decorating mood in my home shifts from simple to exotic, from sentimental to sleek, and everything in between.

# On the Shelf

**Decorating rich** on the shelf is where one lovingly places those personal collections that honor the beauty of everyday objects. Those saved and cherished pieces that are the most important to you and the members of your family. The ones that include anything from old photographs in antique frames to the teacher-inspired handprint wall plaque your son gave you for Christmas in the first grade.

The displaying of such collectibles is like the telling of a story. Depending on how you assemble the cast of characters and set the scenes, you can tell a tale of sunny days spent with "grandma great" at her cottage on the beach, the first day of school with all of its tears and reassuring hugs, or prom night when your husband finally realized his little girl was all grown up.

There are no absolute definitions on what a shelf should be or definitive guidelines on how that which you want displayed should be arranged. All you need is a passion for favorite things and a sense of style that is all your own.

"Shelves" can be created by simply stacking boxes on top of each other. If the boxes become progressively smaller, the spaces in between can be used to display anything from photographs to flower arrangements.

I personally like using the floor as a place to "build" my shelves. The items placed here are easily obtainable and it takes the interest in the room literally from floor to ceiling. This method of decorating, however, is not recommended if there are small children around or if you are a follower of Feng Shui principles.

Many times the items that are collected by collectors are not priceless or memorable or permanent; but they do create a need to have lots of shelf space available on which to display them. To the *lower left* a collection of old suitcases is not only displayed, but adds additional storage space in a small home. *Above* a metal shelf is used as a cornice on top of a window. It is a perfect unexpected shelf to display a collection of candles that is changed with each new holiday or season.

(3) It is much more interesting to take collectibles to new levels by placing items on risers such as wooden boxes, dishes, books, flat-topped baskets, and small benches or chairs. (4) Choose items that you love, otherwise they may simply become that which begins to annoy you because they collect dust and make your rooms feel "crowded and cluttered."

More often than not, the pieces that I display upon my shelves are those that were designed or created by an artisan somewhere in the world. The lamp and the candle stand on the *upper left* are no exception. A friend of mine made these items from leftover candlesticks she found on sale and old mexican lanterns with bright orange glass.

Do not forget that it can be an added *decorating rich* touch to make the shelf as interesting as that which you place upon it. Make your shelf look expensive and like an original work of art by adding strings of beads, tassels, or fabric pieces on the shelf top.

The shelves on the *facing page* have been embellished with beads strung on beading wire. An eclectic style of brightly colored beads add color and interest, while the combination of creamy white and clear beads have an air of sophistication. The beaded style is completed when beads are strung onto tassels and tied onto the shelves. A piece of cardboard can be cut to the shape of the shelf and covered with a rich cut-velvet, brocade, or faux-silk fabric remnant.

74

For reasons that I can not explain, many women love to collect bottles. Sometimes each is filled with matching colored bath crystals and bath oils, or they contain a variety of items used in cooking, or sometimes they are just left empty. Whether you decorate one or every way, they hold a fascination that is simply unexplainable.

We have an artist who takes her collection of bottles a step even further. She is a caterer and in each of the containers she uses in her own kitchen or for her catered parties, she places unusual bottle stoppers. You can often find large crystals that she found on broken chandeliers, beautiful marbles that were picked up in local flea markets, or liquor bottle stops used in tiny pitchers of oils and spices.

In addition to using different tops for your bottles, consider making or buying unusual labels for each. An ordinary canning jar filled with cookies can become a work of art and the perfect gift with a label that is a family photograph. Such labels are now in an overabundant supply in scrapbooking and art supply stores, as well as on discs of computer art. Be creative—a collection of bottles is such fun, can be very inexpensive, and is actually something that is utilitarian.

Both cooks and collectors love jars, bottles, baskets, boxes, or whatever can actually hold items used in cooking on their shelves. I have a friend who is not much of a shopper but is an avid collector and a gourmet cook. She always uses her jars that she has filled with the fruits, vegetables, salsas, and jams as a way of decorating in her kitchen. It is such a treat to see the colors and the fruits of the season on her shelves. Each time I am invited to tea we take one of the bottles from the shelf and enjoy whatever is inside while we discuss the problems of the world and the day's upcoming events. I never turn down one of her invitations because each time I rise to go, she hands me a jar of that which is her current favorite recipe.

*Decorating rich* is not expensive—it is finding a way to decorate with whatever you have, whatever you have created or collected, and whatever is your passion. It is this sort of simple decorating that is most enjoyed and most remembered. Take your favorite things out of the closets and cupboards and drawers and find a place for them where they can be enjoyed by everyone who sees them as much as they are enjoyed by you.

Make an ordinary jar very unordinary by wrapping it in something special. A vintage piece of needlework placed around a bottle and topped off with vintage lace complements whatever the contents may be.

A table napkin can be folded into a triangle and wrapped around a bottle. The napkin can be secured by tucking the corner under the edge. Fold back the point and attach a decorative pin. Glue artificial fruit and leaves to a pin back for your own design.

Plain glass vases that are often received with flower bouquets can be given elements of design ever so simply. All you need do is draw on your imagination; for example, use the same technique you learned in wrapping your child's ponytail to covert a plain glass vase into something noteworthy *(upper right)*. This elegant look is created by wrapping ribbon around a cylindrical vase and interlocking the ribbon ends, then finishing off by knotting the ribbon.

Two women whose artistic talents I envy are Susan Alexander and Taffnie Bogart. They have coauthored a publication for Sterling/Chapelle entitled *Handmade Clay Crafts* and own a gallery to display their art. Both Susan and Taffnie know how to *decorate rich* on the shelf, or anywhere else for that matter. Here, they have taken outdoor clay planters and brought them indoors. By surrounding them with fruits and eggs and flowers from their garden, their decorating on a shelf is natural, homey, and evidence that the simplest choices are never merely afterthoughts, but decisions that make *decorating rich* a reality.

## For the Bath

For most of us, the bath is a place where we go to shower, apply makeup, comb our hair, and leave. But most of us long to make it a place where we can retreat—a personal oasis of quiet indulgence—where warm scented water lulls us into tranquility, and where perfumed oils and soothing lotions smooth away the stresses of modern life.

However small your room, and regardless of how many must share it, decorate it, fill it, and use it

86

as a haven and a retreat to spend precious time.

It may be true that the reality of your busy life is that one morning or evening a month is all of the time that can be found for indulging yourself. However, you can surround yourself—on the shelves of your bath—with a few simple embellishments and stylings that create wonderful evocative mood settings. These items are ready for those moments you do find to pamper both your body and your soul.

Cans filled with fresh-cut flowers, towels wrapped to resemble expensive gifts, beautiful bottles filled with sweet-smelling lotions or indulgent creams, and candles to soften the light and set the mood—these are what should be placed on the shelves of your bath to help in your celebration of ancient rituals.

When *decorating rich* on the bath shelf, remember to use that which is unexpected. I use a fan, purchased long ago on a trip to China town, as the mat for the soap dish—which is, of course, the shell that was found on the beach in Hawaii last summer. Use everything, everywhere—it is what makes *decorating rich* irresistible and essential.

The side of the tub is considered by some, to qualify as a shelf. It is, in fact, the perfect shelf on which to place any item that is an accessory to the pleasures of pampered luxury. Drape a cotton throw in which to wrap yourself in place of a towel. Have a tray filled with glasses for a small sip of wine or sparkling water, greenery to make you feel as if you are in a woodland stream somewhere, and bottles filled with skin-care pleasures.

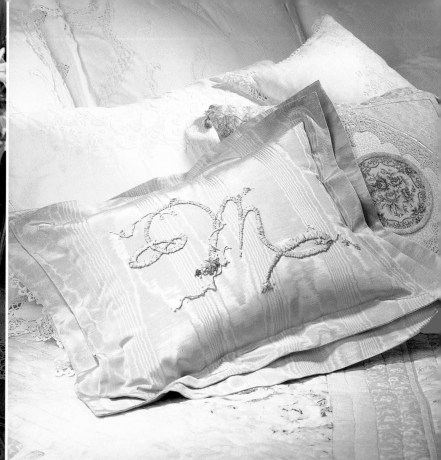

One simple utilitarian object from a bygone era adds a romantic feminine touch to a now very lovely place. One delicately embroidered pillow on the top of a carefully chosen coverlet is all that is needed to set the entire mood in a room. Some such pillows are expensive, some are handmade by you or a friend, and some are found slightly damaged at flea markets and garage sales, but all that is needed is one—it says all that needs to be said in a single glance.

The top of the bed may be the perfect place for nothing but a pillow or two, or several pillows and a throw, or for a small tray that holds an evening snack. It matters not what is put there, as long as you like it.

Even though decorating on the bed with pillows is the most expected decorating style, it can still be one where *decorating rich* is easier than ever. When purchased in either the fine linen or expensive accessory section of department and gift stores pillows can be unaffordable and unimaginative. There are so many ways to make so many inexpensive yet truly beautiful pillows for whatever style bed you may have.

*Below,* you will see a pillow with a color photo transfer. It is easy, elegant, and inexpensive. A favorite piece of art or even a photograph can be photocopied in color and transferred onto fabric, using a photo transfer medium. The pillow is trimmed in a wire-edged ribbon that was whipstitched in place. The pillow was completed by gluing cording around the edge of the art for a frame. The final result is a decorative pillow that is unique in and of itself. Possessing that item that is one of a kind or a signature piece is simply another way of *decorating rich.*

A great basic pillow that can be made and remade is created by rolling up a neckroll pillow or pillow form in a beautiful scarf. Tassled curtain tiebacks are knotted at each open end and an attractive pillow is finished in only a few minutes. This project is simple enough to do and no sewing is required.

When *decorating rich*, it is important to take several elements and put them together in one style statement. In the *upper right,* an inexpensive plain pillow was purchased on a closeout. A remnant of fabric or an old scarf was then used to tie around the pillow to add color, texture, and interest. Tassels were then attached—a number of them—all of which were purchased in a discontinued-style sale at a fabric and decorating store. The total cost was minimal and yet, the effect is very nice indeed.

## Decorating with Storage

Decorating on the bed could be said to include on, underneath, behind, at the foot of, and next to if you are being creative and *decorating rich.* Here are examples of ways to include storage space in the bedroom with no trouble and little expense. Discarded trunks, old suitcases, and a variety of boxes can all hold seasonal clothing, dress items and accessories only occasionally used, holiday decorating items, or almost anything that is not used on a daily basis. When using your storage items and storage space as part of your decor, you have a clear understanding of *decorating rich.*

98

When *decorating rich,* you have the freedom to look at the room as a whole or divide it into small sections. You can use a lot or a little, you can use only that which is essential, or focus on that which is unnecessary. In other words, you can do whatever you choose. When *decorating rich,* there is no right or wrong, acceptable or unacceptable, stylish or unstylish. There is only an essential contentment with what you have chosen and a commitment to your own needs and wants.

## Creating a Private Haven

Turn a small corner of a room into a special area for reading, relaxing, or pampering. It matters not that the furnishings be richly covered with romantic embroidery, they just need to be comfortable and inspirational.

These two rooms are so very different, yet serve exactly the same purpose. They offer a place for private times where your own needs come first and there is no room for self-sacrifice. Let only those enter who respect the reasons why you have created such a haven.

## Doing Something with Nothing

*Decorating rich* is taking nothing and making it look like a lot of something. Here in my bathroom at home, I have created an area that is essential and oftentimes hidden, and made it a "main attraction." The water closet became the "library" with an old door and a new piece of etched glass. The "library" shelves are made with old balusters cut into small pieces, and the hanging lights are clear glass mosaics that have words decoupaged under the glass surface. On either side of the door, two scarves hang. In the bathroom area, itself, is a collection of tiles that I have purchased from excess accumulated by tile stores and tile layers.

Collections are the very core of *decorating rich* because they perform two functions. The first is to own, yourself, that which you love most; and the second is to use something that was purchased for another reason. Here on these two pages are collections of dishes, dolls, and handmade items made by artisan friends of the homeowner. They are collected for emotional reasons, yet are displayed not only for those reasons, but because they are already owned and loved by the homeowner.

A small area can make a big difference if special attention is paid to it. Here at the end of a hall-way—where most do not think to decorate—a small table with two matching chairs and three wall mirrors have been placed. It is an arrangement that is so unexpected it will be remembered by everyone who sees it.

Another aspect of *decorating rich* is to copy what the rich do. Here is an elegant bed with a stately and unusual headboard. If made from the finest silks and created by an expensive designer this small accent can be pricey indeed. However, it can be easily duplicated. Take a large wire ring, attach a scalloped piece of velvet over the ring, and hang fabric purchased at closeout stores down to the floor. The prices for such an item can range from pocket change to a major investment.

The same is true of the draperies to the *left*. A simple curtain rod hung around the bed is draped with sheer fabric. The fabric purchased can be handwoven and hand-dyed . . . or not.

113

# On a Whim

Decorating rich on a whim is the best of all. It is here that you can do whatever you choose. It is the objects in decorating on a whim that make you smile when you enter the room, it is the colors that brighten your mood and lift your soul, and it is the composition or placement that makes you turn and look again. It is decorating that is bright and fresh and welcomes life. It is doing something that breaks all of the rules and that has probably never been done before—or at least never seen by anyone you know.

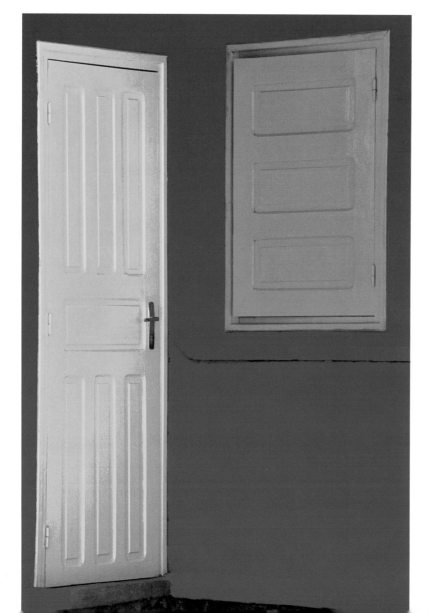

Here, *decorating rich* on a whim is strictly the use of color. When walking down a hallway, why not make it a statement—it is only paint—that you can change whenever you want to. How many mothers wish they could find a reason to keep their children's doors closed and especially the one to the bathroom they use. Well, here is an excuse to do so. If you turn the painted doors in your hall into works of art, it will become essential that they be closed at all times so that the "picture" you have created does not lose any of its impact. Besides it is wonderful, temporary, and inexpensive.

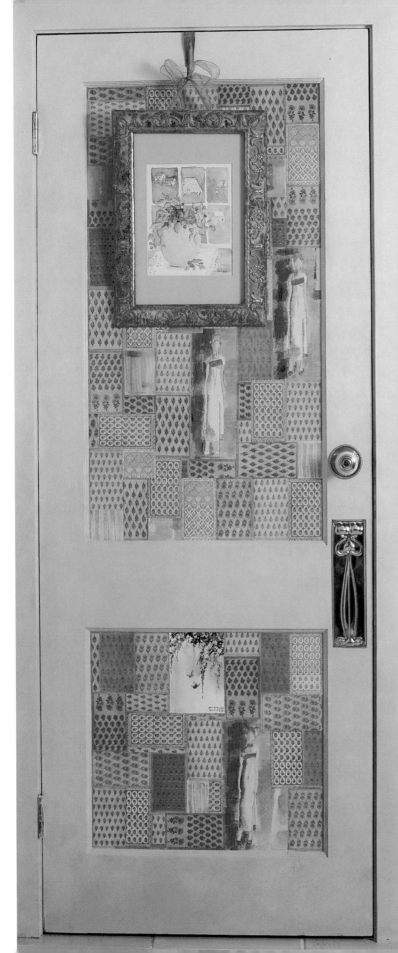

What you hang on your doors can also turn them into a piece of art. The door *(facing page, left)* has a small plaid heart filled with sachet hanging from the knob. Tassels will work, as will small purses. Pictures also can be hung on doors as shown *above.*

*Facing page, upper right:* A hook was attached to the outside of the door and a handmade scarf hangs down the center.

My favorite trick for *decorating rich* on a whim is the knobs on a door—you can use anything or any combination to make your plain cabinet fronts not so plain. To the *left,* a Chapelle artist took her white cabinet doors and added different handles to each. Not only is each handle different, but some doors have two. *Above,* the drawers on this antique filing cabinet were labeled with old cards that have been cut up. No plain brown labels for this artist!

I never cease to be amazed at what people collect and what they do or do not do with their collections.

I had no explanation as to why, but years ago I began collecting Bakelite™ handles. I had no place to use them and no future plans in which they could be included; however, for reasons I was not aware of, I loved them. When my husband and I purchased an old home to renovate, I designed plain bird's-eye maple cabinets which made the perfect home for all of my knobs.

Shortly after moving into our home, I was visiting a nephew. In his garage, I saw an old chest of drawers that had been owned by my grandmother. I suddenly remembered that chest in my grandmother's bedroom, the drawers that were filled with treasures, and the Bakelite handles.

## Decorating with a Theme

*Decorating rich* on a whim can also mean decorating with a theme. Why not take an entire room and make it something from another time and another place.

The man who owns this den is a collector of tramp art. His grandfather had been a casualty of the depression, and during his travels, he had learned the skill of carving. In better times, he taught his son and his grandson how to carve; and even though these are not his pieces, they have a special place in this collector's heart.

It is so rewarding to decorate with a theme, and it need not be through the entire house. The Arts and Crafts movement is very popular, Art Nouveau or Art Deco decorating can be very entertaining, and decorating in a 60s' or 70s' style can give you an explanation for the new décor in your son's bedroom!

127

## Remember the Details

Decorating on a whim is in the details—the finer points. When you look very closely, you see that which you never expected to see.

This birdhouse is indeed beautiful in and of itself, but what caught my eye was the tiny vintage glass wreaths attached to each door. These could be hung from any birdhouse door regardless of how fancy or plain.

The towel to the *left* is part of a bathroom vanity display. What made it most unusual is the use of a brooch that the artist attached to the bottom of the towel. She loved this pin, but hardly ever wore it. By attaching it to the towel, she is able to enjoy it every day.

*Decorating rich* is easy decorating. The picture frame to the *left* was created by one of our artists for her school-age children to give as gifts. She had two pieces of glass cut and sanded at the glass store. She then inserted the photograph between the glass pieces and tied with a ribbon. It is the perfect gift—handmade, meaningful, inexpensive, and can be used singly or in multiples for decorating.

*Facing page, lower left*: Small bunches of potpourri were tied in organdy squares. They are the perfect hostess gift because they, too, are pretty enough to use as decorative accents and they freshen the room as well. Try making them in red and green for the holidays, or use pastel pieces of dotted swiss for a spring bridal shower. Gift-giving, decorating, functional use—all equal *decorating rich.*

Terra-cotta flowerpots are readily available and moderately priced. Besides their color and texture being the perfect coordinating or complementary accessories for almost any decor, they can be used for a variety of things. One flowerpot *(upper left)* was turned upside down, then a matching flowerpot was glued to it. A small glass vase was placed in the upright pot and fresh flowers were added. Three terra-cotta pots *(above)* were used as a stand, while a large terra-cotta saucer was used as the tray for makeup and accessories. The wonderful thing about terra-cotta pots is that they can be painted, stained, or decoupaged to match any style or decor.

131

The simple beauty of small things—I love their intricacy, their understated elegance, and their unessential reason for being. Each of these was made from scraps of fabric and lace. Each selected piece of fabric can be purchased as a remnant in the fabric store or they can be the childhood clothes you cut pieces from to save. Each is as romantic as a sonnet that echoes a more courtly era and gentile time.

*Facing page, upper left:* A romantic fabric-covered box, trimmed with antique lace and fringe, is finished off with the charms from a bracelet the buyer never wore.

*Facing page, upper right:* A fabric topiary speaks of the Victorian period, with a fabric-covered clay pot trimmed with gold braid. A wooden dowel is inserted into a foam ball for the trunk and covered by a rectangular scrap of fabric. Leaves are cut from a remnant of upholstery fabric. Some of the leaf edges are dipped into glue and then into tiny beads before being glued onto the ball. Narrow gold ribbon is twisted and glued around the leaves. The trunk is inserted into a foam block that is adhered to the inside of the flowerpot to complete this lovely vintage-style topiary as an accessory for any table or shelf.

*Facing page, lower left:* Wooden apples covered with small squares of fabric and trimmed with a stem and leaves make rustic accent pieces.

*Facing page, lower right:* Book covers made from vintage lace and fabric pieces are a poetic finish for those treasured books on display.

*Above:* This well-loved, yet seasoned book of sonnets is on exhibit with a sheer ribbon bow and trim, set off by a ribbon rose and leaves.

Search the world for the richness and beauty of faraway places, for the cultural influences and eclectic elements of shape and design, for the unexpected that is to be found everywhere. A *decorating rich* adaptation of oriental simplicity is these bamboo rods that have been placed not only to add support to the ever-fragile orchids, but to give a sense of style to what could be considered by some to be an ordinary arrangement.

136

Photographed by Luciana Pampalone

Photographed by Luciana Pampalone

Few things inspire more than the simple beauty of fresh flowers. The flowers need not be rare and expensive, the arrangements need not be elaborate and difficult to create. All that is needed is the blossoms and colors and scents of the seasons. A bunch of tulips—picked on a beautiful spring day from the garden—placed randomly in a vase can convey feelings of being spirited, confident, comfortable, loving, expressive, peaceful, independent, caring, and playful. It is the true essence of *decorating rich* and loving what you do.

137

With colors and shapes and treasures inspired by the sea, this freshwater aquarium is a vision of what mermaids must see in the deep, under the gentle splash of the early morning waves. The water is clear and clean, and the fish are at home in a pool with translucent hand-blown glass and living plants. Marbles, from long ago, and sea glass found at the water's edge, fill the bottom of the tank where the aquatic inhabitants swim in and out of an aqua-colored glass fish and a dish that holds a delicate clam shell.

To create such a water wonderland for your fish, you first must acclimate them to this new environment. Wash each item thoroughly, place in the tank with hardier breeds of fish for several days. Add your more exotic fish later.

You may also fill your fish bowl with the shells that have been collected on summer days.

139

The collecting of "things" is essential to *decorating rich.* The pieces may be expensive and, therefore, collected one at a time on special occasions; or they may be like items found in a dollar store, whose bargain price was irresistible. The glasses *above*—each different—were individual gifts for memorable days or found while traveling to new unseen places. The fireplace tiles on the *facing page* are such a collection.

Make part of your home a reflection of the "art and soul" of you. Surround yourself with the "pretty" things that are needed when you spend hour upon hour doing that which inspires you, satisfies you, and makes you whole.

How could you possibly capture the beauty of the flowers in the garden if your paints are stored in old brown boxes and your apron is a tattered hand-me-down shirt? You must create the entire illusion, complete with fancy bottles filled with paint, a carrier that transports any-

thing from garden seed to much loved brushes, and an apron that is painted with the beauty of last year's pansies.

If you are a potter, use your beginning pieces to hold brushes, paints, and glazes. Work in front of a window to let the sunshine in or to better hear the gently falling rain.

If you are a gardener, decorate your hat with the fruits of your labors. Use inexpensive wooden shelves or racks to hold your seeds.

For some, the buying, the planning, and the thinking about doing is as satisfying and fulfilling as the actual doing. I have a sewing room in my home that is decorated, adorned, and supplied with all that is essential in creating beautiful pieces of wearable art. I have antique fabrics that I have collected, I have wonderful baskets filled with beads and trims and buttons, I have patterns and designs I purchased for ideas, I have antique sewing boxes filled with the finest silk threads, and I even have my grandmother's sewing machine set up and ready to use. It is just that I never do use it. I spend many a rainy afternoon in this room feeling the fabrics, enjoying my collection of beads and buttons, designing and creating new designs—and for me it is enough. This room, filled with its unused but much-loved treasures, brings me comfort and quiet on a day when my world is like a runaway train. It offers contentment on weekends when my family and friends are busy or away, and most of all, it inspires me for the days to come.

146

Stairways have always been important in any stately manor and thus are designed to be ornate, overdone, and expensive. However, when *decorating rich,* it is the unexpected detail in this ordinary place that delights and inspires.

My husband is a passionate lover of baseball, so of course, the railing in his sportsden had to be authentic major league bats. I wish I could have you hear the sheer delight in every man's voice who enters this room!

If a romantic mood is more what you desire, why not add a simple candleholder to the foot of a simple wrought-iron railing? During the cold winter evenings as your guests don their coats to leave, they will depart with a warm feeling in their hearts.

Your stairway need not be the most costly architectural element in your home to be that which is the most unusual and most welcoming.

There are places in every home that often seem ordinary and unimportant, but it is just these places that are perfect to begin *decorating rich.* Because paint is usually the most manageable, the most affordable, and the most easily changed, why not paint that special something in someplace usually forgotten.

On the *facing page*, the floor and the back wall down a long unused hallway, were painted with a fantasy rug and shelf. An actual mirror was hung above the shelf, completing the illusion. On the *upper right,* the walls in this garden room were aged and painted two colors to accentuate the worn brick floor. On the *lower right,* the laundry room floor was faux-finished to look like tile. Vintage drawers and tables were added, and this room became one that is not only used often, but enjoyed.

When *decorating rich,* every room, every detail, everywhere needs to be designed, completed, and enjoyed.

# On the Outside

On the outside—is it the first place you decorate or the last? Is it the most important or the least? It is, after all, that which you see the least, but that which the rest of the world sees the most. It is the cover of the book by which you are oftentimes judged.

The outside is often left undone due to the expense, the enormity, and the transitory nature of the seasonal elements. It is, however, one of many places that *decorating rich* gives you a place and an opportunity to create from what is at hand.

The outside of a home that is vibrant with color and texture, awash with light, and simply furnished with hand-painted wooden furniture is an opportunity to enhance your life—wherever you choose to live.

It is in this time and place that a home becomes a setting for self-expression and a return to simplicity. *Decorating rich* on the outside can be a statement of love for natural materials, pared-down content, a looser approach to ornamentation, and a bolder use of color. Live life well, combine this new and generous attitude of decorating the outside of your home with a similar exuberance for the life you lead within it.

*Decorating rich* on the outside can be very similar to the style you use on the inside of your home. What you wish for most is a place that offers a warm welcome for family, friends, and strangers; a peaceful place to relax and enjoy each other or the quiet and colors of nature; a simple open place to work, and plant, and play. It is here, after all, that we can forget about what goes on in other times and other places and be either an adult or a child—again and again.

When *decorating rich* on the outside, the use of colors and materials is most effective when defined by nature. There is no more beautiful a "picture" in a once drab place than flowers that bloom through the summer season, or no table that welcomes conversation and family gatherings more than one made from the rough logs of the tree that—before it was toppled by the wind—was once growing tall and strong in the backyard.

The ornaments you use on the outside of the home should alter the mood of all who enjoy them, provoke the thoughts of all who take the time to see them, and induce a feeling of calm for all who spend time among them.

When "decorating" the outside of the house, it is certain that it needs to be practical so that it can be used and enjoyed, but it need not be ordinary and uninteresting. Paint your cedar swing in the backyard the color of a summer sky and add French country pillows. Replace a standard director's chair seat and back with small pieces saved from an old quilt. And for the furniture on the porch, throw an afghan which will be there to keep you warm on cool autumn evenings.

154

156

Even I, who live my entire life by the philosophy that "too much is never enough," have places in my garden where the simplicity of one favored piece is all that is needed. I never cease to be amazed at the impact of a single stone statue or a lone rocking chair, when placed in the midst of the miracles of nature. There is no sight more wondrous than sitting quietly on my patio and watching as the birds pause to spend a minute or two. It makes me return to that in life which is not only simple, but is all that is really important.

# Index

# Acknowledgments

The publishers wish to thank the following for use of their projects, homes, businesses, or photographs:

Susan Alexander and Taffnie Bogart: pp 82/83, 84, 85(u)(br), 142

Artville, LLC Images (© 1997, 1998): pp 7(bl), 8, 9, 10(ul), 11(bl), 12(ul), 17(r), 41(u), 46(ur), 67(b), 69(r), 90, 106(ur), 112(ul)(r)(bl), 113(u), 149(u)

Beehive House: p 46(ul)(br)

Brigham Street Inn: p 155

Corbis Corporation Images (© 1999): pp 18(ul), 24/25, 58, 73(r), 158(ur)

Digital Stock Corporation (© 1997): pp 6(br), 60(b), 114, 115, 116/117, 151(ul), 151(bl)

Dixie Barber: pp 20(bl), 33(bl), 35, 36(br), 37, 76, 135(u)(br)

Susan and Boyd Bingham; p 91

Pat and Clyde Buehler: p 89(br)

Anita Louise Crane: p 132(ul)

Diana Dunkley: pp 130, 131(bl), 132(ur)(bl)

Linda Durbano: pp 25(br), 26(l)(r), 27, 28(ul)(bl)(r), 29(l), 30(bl)(r), 32, 33(ul), 42, 65, 67(u), 106(bl), 107(bl), 122, 129(b)

Kathryn Elliott: pp 10(bl), 14(ul), 16(ur), 113(l)

Lisa Eyre: p 105

Joan B. Hall: p 86(u)

Ryne Hazen: p 77(u)

Sue Henshaw: p 2(l)

Hobo & Tramp Art: pp 69(l), 126, 127

Debra and David Johnson: p 45

MacKenzie-Childs Ltd.: pp 28(r), 49(r), 110

McKenzie Kate: p 81(b)

Marni Kissel: pp 29(r), 73(m), 74(ul)

Shannon McBride: pp 7(br), 74(bl), 147(r)

Jo Packham: pp 2(r), 4, 22(ul), 60(u), 62(u)(b), 63, 66(ul)(b), 68, 73(u)(b), 75(l)(br), 81(ul)(ur), 86(b), 94(ul)(ur)(b), 96(l)(r), 97(ur)(b), 98(ur)(b), 99, 100, 101(ul)(bl)(br), 107(u), 108(br), 109(u)(bl)(br), 110, 111(br), 118, 120(l)(ur), 121(l)(r), 123, 124, 125, 128, 129(u), 134, 138/139, 139, 140, 141(l)(r), 146

Luciana Pampalone: pp 1, 3, 70, 71, 103, 136, 137

Robert Perron: pp 13(br), 34, 148

Photodisc, Inc. Images (© 1995, 1999, 2000): pp 6(ur), 10(ul), 11(u), 12(ur), 13(ur)(ul)(um), 14(ur)(br)(bl), 15(ul)(bl)(m)(ur), 20(ul)(ur), 21(b), 44(u)(b), 46(bl), 47(br), 48(u)(b), 50(ul)(br)(ur), 51(br)(bl)(ul), 52, 53(ur)(br)(ul)(bl), 54, 55(bl)(br)(ur), 59(u)(br)(bl), 72, 78(u)(b), 85(bl), 98(ul), 104(br), 106(br), 108(u), 147(m)(l), 150(u)(b), 151(br)(ur), 152(ur)(br), 153(ur)(ul)(b), 156(ul)(br)(ur)(bl), 158(ur), 159(u)(l)

Pat Poce: pp 7(br), 74(b), 147(r)

Rhonda Rainey: p 16(ul)(b)

Mike and Julie Reeske: p 131(ur)

Sharon Stasney: pp 33(r), 56(ul)(r)(bl), 57, 101(ur), 104(ul), 105, 149(b)

Edie Stockstil: pp 22(bl), 80(u)(b), 154(u)(b)

Sara Toliver: p 149(b)

Trends and Traditions: pp 77(b), 143(r)

Susan Ure, Floribunda: pp 24(bl), 25(ur), 41(br), 119

Ward and Child: pp 43(r), 56(ul)(r)(bl), 57, 101(ur), 104(ul)

Washington School Inn: p 95(ul)

Susan Whitelock: pp 79, 116(l), 145

Fontelle Young: pp 6(ur), 40, 120(br)

Scot Zimmerman: pp 31(u)(b), 36(u)(bl), 38(u)(bl)(br), 39, 43(l), 55(l), 64, 66(r), 92(u)(ur)(m)(b), 93, 102, 104(ur), 106(ul), 111(u)(bl)